THE
ULTIMATE
HALF LOG CABIN BOOK

by Sharyn Craig

CHITRA PUBLICATIONS

Your Best Value in Quilting!
www.QuiltTownUSA.com

First Printing: 2001

Library of Congress Cataloging-in-Publication Data

Craig, Sharyn Squier, 1947-
   The ultimate half log cabin quilt book / by Sharyn Craig.
     p. cm.
   ISBN 1-885588-40-2
   1. Patchwork—Patterns. 2. Log cabin quilts.   I. Title.
TT835 .C73324 2001
746.46'041—dc21

2001032508

Edited by: Nancy Roberts
Design and Illustrations: K.A. Steele
Inside Photogaphy: Carina Woolrich Photography, San Diego, California

OUR MISSION STATEMENT

We publish quality quilting magazines and books
that recognize, promote, and inspire self-expression.
We are dedicated to serving our customers with
respect, kindness, and efficiency.

Introduction

I made my first Half Log Cabin quilt in 1989. It was inspired by a quilt shown in Laura Fisher's book *Quilts of Illusion* (Sterling Publishing, 1988). That quilt, named "Hayes Corner," was made circa 1930 by an Amish quiltmaker. Since my first quilt made in that style, I have made so many Half Log Cabin and Logs Plus quilts that I have truly lost count!

The Half Log Cabin pattern became the focus of my 1991 "Design Challenge" feature in *Traditional Quiltworks* magazine, Issue 14. Four years later, quilting friend Carolyn Smith asked a question that prompted a whole new series of Half Log Cabin quilts. After seeing rows of triangles added to traditional Log Cabin blocks, she wondered if it was possible to add them to Half Log Cabin blocks. I explored an answer to her question that resulted in the Logs Plus design variation. It became the "Design Challenge" featured in *Traditional Quiltworks*, Issue 51.

These "Design Challenges" are a great way to showcase a concept and present lots of quilt variations made possible by changing the block layout and coloring. Because the availability of magazines is limited and because the designs were so popular, my books *Half Log Cabin Quilts* and *Half Log Cabin Plus* were published in 1996 and 1998, respectively.

Perhaps you're wondering, "Why a new book?" Well, to be honest, I can never leave anything alone! One of my strong points as a teacher is in finding easy, organized, and efficient methods for sewing. At the time that the magazine articles were published, I presented really slick methods to sew the blocks. Later, I fine-tuned, streamlined, and perfected the methods even more and offered them in the books. Now, I have further polished, tweaked, and simplified the techniques.

Most of the quilts in this book are new. A couple of the ones that were shown in my earlier books were so special and unique that I truly felt you'd want to see them. In this book, I'm offering more information, showing you more quilts, and sharing more ideas. I'm also providing new and improved instructions.

I have been teaching both Half Log Cabin and Logs Plus in national and international workshops for many years. Whenever I teach, I look for new ways to express concepts so they become easier for students to understand. I learn from them and strive to be a better teacher every time I'm in the classroom. You'll find the benefits of all that practice and experience in this book.

The Chevron Log Cabin is a brand new addition. The basic block is stitched in the the same manner as the other blocks, but the way it is colored makes it look different. The Chevron block tradition-

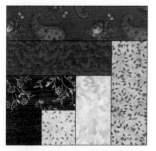

Half Log Cabin

Logs Plus

Chevron Block

ally starts with a bright square (often red) and then progresses from the lightest to the darkest value strips, in a "V" formation.

Coloration has a major impact on the look of the quilts. Both Half Log Cabin and Logs Plus blocks rely on light and dark fabrics placed to visually split the block in half diagonally.

Because all three patterns are included in this book, the visual stimulation provided by the photos is sure to inspire you. There are no limits to the directions you can take when it comes to laying out your blocks. That's why I encourage you to be creative. If you see a layout for a Half Log Cabin quilt in colors that you love, but you'd prefer to make Logs Plus blocks, then combine the ideas from both designs into your own unique version.

When you are ready to make your first quilt using this book, I urge you to select a wide variety of prints which I call "working scrappy." Doing so means you will never run out of fabric no matter what size you make your quilt. I often start a quilt planning to make a small 24-block project. But as soon as I discover how much I like the results, I want to make a bigger quilt. If I was working with a select group of prints, making a bigger quilt might not be possible because the amount of each fabric in my stash is limited. Working scrappy doesn't mean you have to ignore color. Your quilt can be just one color and still be scrappy. The difference is that a controlled green quilt might be made from half a dozen prints, while a scrap green quilt could be made from 60 different ones.

Chapter 1 has a single block diagram that can be used when making any of the quilts. It also has a chart that shows three block sizes and the different strip widths to cut when making each size. If you are making your first Half Log Cabin, Logs Plus, or Chevron quilt, I suggest using 2" wide strips to make 6" finished blocks.

I like 2" strips and keep boxes of them on hand. I cut a 2" strip from each fabric that is on my cutting table for any reason. Then I group strips by color and store them in shoe boxes. You might prefer to sort the strips only by light and dark values. That way you'll be ready to sew whenever inspiration strikes. Having an assortment of 2" strips already cut is a great motivator and a time saver.

The patterns and instructions in this book can be used independently of each other. While the quilts are presented in the order in which I worked with each design, you can make them in any order you like. Each of three chapters contains a pattern for a "Project Quilt". It isn't necessary to limit yourself to that specific project, however. For example, you might begin with the 36 blocks in "Half Log Cabin Barn Raising" (page 9). As you work with the blocks, you may decide you prefer a different layout. Several possibilities are illustrated in Chapter 4. What if you want your quilt larger than 36 blocks? No problem! The beautiful freedom of working scrappy allows you to simply add more strips to the pile and keep piecing.

A gallery of quilts made with the same block accompanies each project quilt. Some are simple variations; oth-

ers are exciting "what ifs." I love surprises. Often I substitute other pieced or appliquéd blocks for some of the Log Cabin ones. Sometimes I add appliqués to the quilt surface. There are several examples like this in each chapter. The blocks in this book not only make great quilts on their own, they are also wonderful support blocks to combine with others. Experiment with blocks you have on hand. For example, you don't have to use Crazy Five-Pointed Stars and a Crow block when inspired by "Something to Crow About" (page 23). Perhaps you have some Sawtooth Stars and a Sunbonnet Sue block. Use them instead. Anything can work if you let those creative ideas flow!

As a quilter since 1978, I know how easy it is to fall into making a quilt the expected or "normal" way. I'm referring not only to sewing techniques, but also to the coloration and layout. Often, when we know what something is supposed to look like, it is much harder to be creative. Keep an open mind and have a sense of adventure when looking through this book. Then, make sure your sewing machine is in good working order and there is a sharp blade in your rotary cutter, so you'll be ready to sew. I wish you lots of fun and new quilts!

Sharyn

My thanks go to all of the students who have taken my workshops over the years. Their questions and comments have been wonderfully insightful to me. A special thank you goes to the quilters who allowed me to use their quilts in this book. I'm also grateful to the On Call Quilters. This group of dedicated quilters agreed to make quilts especially for this book. When I needed lots more variations of the Chevron Log Cabin quilts than I had time to make, they really came through. I said, "Have fun" and turned them loose with only the block diagram and basic coloring parameters. The results were exciting, and there were even a couple of quilts I would never have recognized as Chevrons! Linda Packer, Carolyn Smith, Marnie Santos, Laurine Leeke, Sandy Andersen, Ruth Gordy, and Margret Reap are so inventive and were able to create spectacular quilts from that simple little block. Thank you also to Joanie Keith who does much of my machine quilting. It's not easy to admit that I cannot do it all, but thanks to these wonderful and supportive quilters I don't have to!

Basic Information

Before you begin sewing, it's a good idea to read through the following sections. In them, I share my tips, preferences, and recommendations that will ensure your success in making Half Log Cabin, Logs Plus, and Chevron quilts. You'll also find my directions for "scrambling" in order to avoid repeating fabric placement in any Half Log Cabin or Logs Plus blocks. Charts provide easy reference for strip widths and lengths.

SUPPLIES

• Sewing machine–Be sure to clean, oil, and replace the needle before beginning any new project.

• Basic sewing supplies–In addition to high quality, 100% cotton thread, you'll need a small scissors for cutting threads. I recommend 50 wt. thread. Using this fine cotton thread is important for the life of your quilts and sewing machine.

• Rotary cutter–I recommend cleaning, oiling, and changing the blade in your rotary cutter. This essential tool can build up a deposit of lint from cutting cotton fabric. You'll want the blade sharp and able to turn freely when cutting. Follow these steps to prepare your rotary cutter:

1. Loosen the nut and the screw and take the cutter apart.
2. Carefully wipe off any lint residue on the blade and cutter.
3. While reassembling the tool, place one drop of sewing machine oil between the blade and the cutter.
4. Place the nut on the screw and tighten it. Avoid over-tightening which will inhibit the blade from turning. You should not have to put any pressure on the cutter to make the blade turn. Try rolling it on just the mat, without fabric, to see if it is adjusted properly.

• Cutting mat

• Clear acrylic rulers–My favorite sizes are 6" x 12" and 4" x 14" for cutting logs, and 4" x 8" for pre-cutting logs for any blocks up to 7 1/2" square (finished size). The important thing is to choose a ruler that you find easy to work with. For instance, you probably won't want to fight with a 24"-long ruler when you're only working with short strips.

• Masking tape–I suggest purchasing 1/4"-wide tape. This size is extremely helpful when pre-cutting logs or sewing diagonally across the small squares used for Logs Plus quilts.

FABRIC

I recommend using 100% cotton prints for the logs. Prints camouflage piecing discrepancies better than solid fabrics can.

While color may be the first thing we notice when looking at a quilt, the value of your fabrics is even more important. Value is how light or dark a fabric "reads" or looks when compared to others. Half Log Cabin and Logs Plus quilts rely on the block being divided diagonally with light strips on one side and dark ones on the other side.

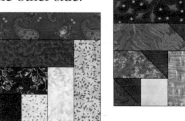

Coloring the block this way creates the same effect as piecing a square from one light and one dark triangle. When you place the divided blocks next to each other and then turn and rotate them, you create different patterns and illusions. If values are too similar from one side to the other, you will be unable to create the same illusions. If you mix light and dark values on both sides, you will also be unable to visually divide the block in half. For instance, when you want to make a blue and yellow quilt, you may choose light, medium, and dark blue strips for one half of the block, and light, medium, and dark yellow strips for the other half of the block. The illustration shows why this is unsuccessful.

You can see how the division of the block into light and dark is broken up. Blocks pieced this way will result in an indistinct pattern on your finished quilt. Unless this is your intention, I recommend keeping the values separated on opposite sides of the block.

Value placement is also critical when piecing Chevron blocks. However, this time the strips graduate from light to dark. The shortest strips are usually the lightest and the longest strips are the darkest. Normally when making Chevron blocks, the same fabric strip is used twice. Note in the numbered diagram that the strips next to the Corner Square in Positions 1 and 2 are cut from the same light print; those in Positions 3 and 4 are cut from the same, slightly darker fabric, and so on. Finally, the strips in Positions 7 and 8 are cut from the same dark fabric.

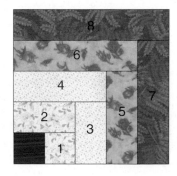

One category of fabric that you may find difficult to work with is multi-colored, large-scale prints such as florals. They often have both light and dark values within the same fabric. When you cut these fabrics into strips, it becomes difficult to determine if they are light or dark. When you place one of them in the dark half of the block the strip may happen to include a light patch which can disrupt the pattern.

COLOR

Even though you are working scrappy, you can still have a specific color recipe for your quilt. Using the example of a blue and yellow quilt again, consider not limiting cut strips to just blue and yellow ones. Instead, stretch that palette by including some green or blue-violet fabrics. If you keep these additional colors in the same tones that your blue strips are, they will lend support to the blues and make them look even better.

To get a better feel for this, study the photos throughout the book. Look at a quilt and decide what color you think it is. Then look more closely at the individual fabrics used. You may be surprised by their range of colors. Begin by looking at the "Barn Raising on Point" Logs Plus quilt on page 22. It reads like a blue and yellow quilt. The yellow used for the small triangles cannot be denied because it is a strong accent. But the quilt became predominantly blue when I chose a blue fabric for the border. It may surprise you to learn that there are very few blue strips in the logs. Actually, there are a lot of black, brown, green, and purple prints used. After sewing the blocks together, I auditioned many different colors with which to frame the quilt with borders, including brown, black, and green. I finally selected blue because it worked well with the yellow triangles.

A look at "Window of Opportunity," a Logs Plus variation quilt on page 23, will probably convince you that the quilt is black. The black sashing strips and black borders reinforce this. Now look at the Logs Plus project quilt in Chapter 3 (page 17). I planned to make it a green and yellow quilt. When cutting strips for the green half of the block, I cut about 24 assorted green print strips and added 12 strips cut from blue and purple fabric. The quilt reads as a green quilt, but the other colors add life and interest to it.

Imagine yourself working scrappy to make blocks with lights on one side and darks on the other. With this as your fabric recipe, use any and all colors that fit into that format. You'll notice that some colors like red and orange tend not to fall in either the dark or light category, so you may need to be careful about using them. For example, if a red strip "pops up" in a selection of blue, brown, green, and purple strips, you've created an attention getter or "zinger." This is not always a good thing because it can interrupt the overall design. However, you may be able to find the "right red" which adds pizzazz to your blocks when used in moderation. The more you understand about color and the more confident you feel about choosing colors, the less you'll need these guidelines.

FABRIC STRIPS

You have several options for strip widths and block sizes. I've provided a chart in this chapter that contains three choices of strip widths and six choices of block dimensions. Blocks finish from 4" square to 9" square, depending on strip width and the number of log positions. The diagram shows that up to 10 logs can be stitched to complete a block. The chart also indicates the precut mea-surement for each log position.

For exact cutting dimensions for a specific block size:

To determine the exact amount of a specific fabric to use, simply add the length of all of the precut logs you want to cut from it. Then, add 2" to the total to be safe.

Here's an example:

1. Assume you are using 2"-wide strips to make 6" finished Half Log Cabin blocks. Refer to the block diagram (page 8) and you'll note that a block labeled X is what you'll be making. According to the diagram, it has logs in six positions. You want to place a dark fabric in Position 6. Assume you want that same fabric to appear this way in 5 blocks.

2. Refer to the chart at the top of page 8 and find the column for 2"-wide strips. Read down the left side of the chart to find Position 6.

3. Slide your finger over to where the columns intersect. For a block made with 2"-wide strips, you'll see that these logs are cut 6 1/2" long.

5. Multiply this by the number of blocks in which you want the same fabric to appear. In this case, 6 1/2" x 5 = 32 1/2".

8. Add 2" to this number for safety. The result is 34 1/2".

9. Divide the result by the number of useable inches in your fabric (usually 40"-42") to determine how many strips to cut. In this case, you'll discover that you get the logs you need from one crosswise strip of fabric.

For cutting the "no-math" way:

Simply determine the number of blocks you want to make and cut one strip of dark and one of light for each. When making 36 blocks, cut 36 light and 36 dark strips. For 80 blocks, cut

80 of each. This will yield more fabric than you need, but it's easy and fast for quilters who don't want to deal with calculating fabric requirements.

PRECUTTING THE LOGS

After cutting fabric strips, segment them by cutting various lengths from them for different positions. Again, let the chart and the block diagram on page 8 be your guide.

As an example, a 6" finished Half Log Cabin block made using 2"-wide strips (Block X on the chart) requires 2", 3 1/2" and 5" segments of light (Positions 1, 3, and 5). It also needs 2", 3 1/2", 5", and 6 1/2" lengths of dark (Corner square and Positions 2, 4, and 6).

I recommend working with four strips at a time. While it's possible to cut through more than four strips, I find this number to be one that provides accuracy and is suited to all quilters. Here's how to cut the segments:

• Position four different strips on the cutting mat, right sides up and one on top of another.

• Align the ends and long sides of the strips.

• Refer to the diagrams to determine where to begin. Right-handed quilters should start cutting at the left end of the strips while left-handed quilters should work from the right.

Right-handed cutting position

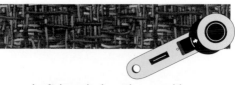
Left-handed cutting position

• Trim the ends of the strips to remove selvages and even the strips.

• Working from the cut edge, cut the required lengths from the strips.

2"   3 1/2"   5"

2"   3 1/2"   5"   6 1/2"

SCRAMBLING

In some of the projects, the instructions will direct you to scramble the logs. Scrambling is a method I use to avoid creating any blocks that contain a fabric in the same position and from creating any blocks that are exactly alike. Position the piles of logs and then follow the directions to either leave the pile alone or move the appropriate num-

ber of logs from the top of the pile to the bottom. So, if the directions tell you to place the two top strips at the bottom, you merely pick up the top two strips and slip them under the bottom one in the pile. Scrambling in this manner means that you will not even have to think about which fabric you're picking up while sewing. The logs will be correctly positioned automatically, and you won't need your seam ripper!

While there is more than one way to make these blocks, I feel that my methods are the most clear and accurate ones. If you decide to try a different way later, it's important to use whatever method you choose consistently.

OTHER FABRIC STRIP INFORMATION

The fabric length required for some positions is quite small. Therefore, you may want to use leftover strips that are smaller than the 42" ones you get by cutting fabric crosswise. The "Half Log Cabin and Logs Plus" chart on page 8 includes my recommendations for total strip lengths to work with when cutting

CUTTING TIP

Make precutting the logs easier with masking tape on your ruler. Adhere a length of 1/4"-wide masking tape to your ruler, as shown. Using a permanent pen, make marks on the tape at the 2", 3 1/2", 5", and 6 1/2" positions.

After evening up the ends of the strips, move the ruler from one mark to the next, cutting the required pieces. You won't have to remember numbers, and you'll always cut the correct sizes.

logs for Half Log Cabin and Logs Plus blocks. The "Chevron Half Log Cabin" chart shows the lengths to work with for the Chevron Half Log Cabin blocks.

NOTE: For Half Log Cabin and Logs Plus blocks, the Corner square (C) and all of the even numbers are dark. All of the odd numbers are light.

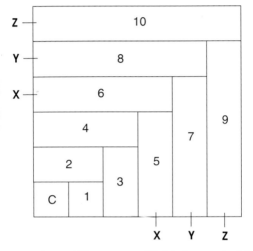

For Chevron Half Log Cabin blocks, C is a bright accent fabric. Each of the following positions are cut from the same fabric: Positions 1 and 2 (usually the same light fabric), Positions 3 and 4 (usually medium light), Positions 5 and 6 (usually medium), Positions 7 and 8 (usually medium dark) and Positions 9 and 10 (usually dark). If you are sewing Chevron blocks with fewer than 10 positions, just shade the blocks from lightest to darkest.

Block Sizes and Precut Logs
Instructions for Half Log Cabin, Logs Plus, and Chevron Blocks

FINISHED BLOCKS

	1 1/2"	1 3/4"	2"
Strip Width	1 1/2"	1 3/4"	2"
Block X	4"	5"	6"
Block Y	5"	6 1/4"	7 1/2"
Block Z	6"	7 1/2"	9"

PRECUT LOG SIZES

C (Corner Square)	1 1/2"	1 3/4"	2"
Position 1	1 1/2"	1 3/4"	2"
Position 2	2 1/2"	3"	3 1/2"
Position 3	2 1/2"	3"	3 1/2"
Position 4	3 1/2"	4 1/4"	5"
Position 5	3 1/2"	4 1/4"	5"
Position 6	4 1/2"	5 1/2"	6 1/2"
Position 7	4 1/2"	5 1/2"	6 1/2"
Position 8	5 1/2"	6 3/4"	8"
Position 9	5 1/2"	6 3/4"	8"
Position 10	6 1/2"	8"	9 1/2"

Half Log Cabin and Logs Plus
Recommended strip lengths for cutting light (L) and dark (D) logs

	STRIP WIDTH					
	1 1/2"		1 3/4"		2"	
	L	D	L	D	L	D
Block X	9"	14"	11"	16"	12"	19"
Block Y	14"	20"	16"	23"	18"	29"
Block Z	19"	26"	23"	31"	28"	40"

Chevron Half Log Cabin
Recommended strip lengths for cutting light (L) and dark (D) logs for up to 10 positions

	STRIP WIDTH		
	1 1/2"	1 3/4"	2"
Positions 1 & 2	6"	7"	8"
Positions 3 & 4	8"	9"	10"
Positions 5 & 6	10"	12"	13"
Positions 7 & 8	12"	14"	16"
Positions 9 & 10	14"	17"	19"

CHAPTER 2

Half Log Cabin Quilts

*PROJECT QUILT- **Half Log Cabin Barn Raising** (48 1/2" square)*

This Project Quilt is a variation of a traditional Barn Raising setting. It's made from thirty-six 6" finished blocks. The blocks are pieced using 2"-wide strips. When you make yours, refer to the quilt photo or the layout diagrams in Chapter 4 to arrange the blocks. Or, choose another layout for your blocks if you prefer. The borders of the quilt shown frame the blocks simply and are made using 2"-wide and 5"-wide strips. You may wish to vary the border in your project. Look through the quilts shown in the Half Log Cabin Gallery in this chapter (pages 12-16) as well as quilts shown in other chapters. Mixing and matching design elements from a variety of sources is fun.

Project Quilt— **Half Log Cabin Barn Raising**

QUILT SIZE: 48 1/2" square
BLOCK SIZE: 6" square

MATERIALS

Yardage is based on 44" fabric with a useable width of 42".

- 36 different dark value prints
- 36 different light value prints
- 3/8 yard inner border fabric
- 1 1/2 yards outer border fabric
- 53" square of batting
- 53" square of backing

CUTTING

Dimensions include a 1/4" seam allowance.

- Cut 36: 2" x 19" strips, dark prints
- Cut 36: 2" x 12" strips, light prints
- Cut 2: 2" x 42" strips, inner border print
- Cut 2: 2" x 40" strips, inner border print
- Cut 2: 5" x 52" lengthwise strips, outer border print
- Cut 2: 5" x 42" lengthwise strips, outer border print
- Cut 5: 2 1/2" x 44" lengthwise strips, outer border print, for the binding

DIRECTIONS

Precut the logs

Refer to Chapter 1 for more information on precutting, as needed.

- Stack 4 dark strips on your cutting mat, rights sides up and long edges aligned. Even the ends, cutting off the selvages.
- Cut these segments from the strips, cutting through all four layers: 2", 3 1/2", 5", 6 1/2". These are Corner Squares and dark logs.
- Cut segments from the remaining dark strips in the same manner.

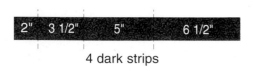

2" 3 1/2" 5" 6 1/2"

4 dark strips

- Position 4 light strips on the mat, aligning and trimming the ends as

you did for the dark ones.
- Cut these segments from the strips: 2", 3 1/2", 5". These are light logs.
- Cut segments from the remaining light strips in the same manner.

2" 3 1/2" 5"

4 light strips

SCRAMBLE THE STRIPS

Refer to Chapter 1 for more information on scrambling, as needed.

- Follow the instructions in the diagram to scramble both the light and dark logs. The numbers refer to the positions of each log in the block and the sewing order. "C" refers to the Corner Square. Note that the Corner Squares and Log 1 are not scrambled.

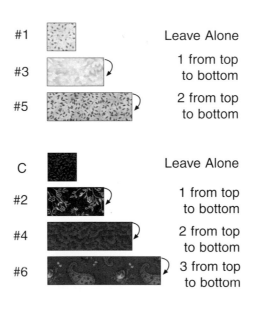

#1	Leave Alone
#3	1 from top to bottom
#5	2 from top to bottom
C	Leave Alone
#2	1 from top to bottom
#4	2 from top to bottom
#6	3 from top to bottom

MANAGEABLE PIECING TIP

While I prefer to work with each pile of 4 logs to yield 4 blocks at a time, the scrambling method is the same regardless of how many logs you work with. Try 8 or 16, or even work with all 36 for this project. Following my scrambling directions will result in unique blocks whether you work with 4 or 400 segments.

Lay out the blocks for sewing

- Keeping the order of each pile intact, lay out logs for the blocks at the left of your sewing machine, following the diagram. Logs 1, 3, and 5 are light, and Logs 2, 4, and 6 are dark.

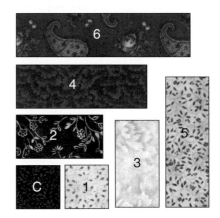

- The block always begins with the Corner Square in the lower left. Light logs are all on the right side of the block while dark ones appear on the left side of the block.

FABRIC TIP

Often quilters have fewer light value prints than dark ones in their collections. If this is the case with you, consider using the same light fabric for more than one block. Or, check the wrong side of dark and medium value strips to see if they look light. If so, use them wrong side up as light strips. I often use the right side of a fabric in one set of blocks and the wrong side of the same fabric in another set. The wrong side of medium value fabrics can be especially successful when used as light strips.

SEW THE BLOCKS

- Take a dark Corner Square and a 2" light square from the piles and place them in front of the sewing machine as shown in the diagram. Be sure they are positioned so that the Corner Square is on the right (R) and light square (Log 1) is on the left (L).

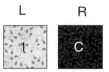

- Place R on top of L, right sides together. To chain sew the units, stitch the squares together along the right edge and stop, leaving the needle and the presser foot down and the unit in the machine.
- Pick up the next two squares from the same piles and sew them, leaving them in the machine as before. Chain sew the remaining Corner Squares and light squares in the same manner.
- Remove the units from the machine. Beginning with the last unit sewn, clip the thread between units, and stack the unopened units so that the first one sewn is now on top.

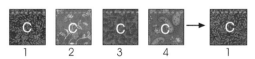

- Turn the entire stack over so that the last unit is now on top and the last segment sewn (Log 1) is visible. Keep the seamline at the top, away from your body.
- Starting with the unit on top, lift Log 1 (last segment sewn) to open the unit and finger press the seam allowance toward it (away from the Corner Square). Repeat with the

remaining units, stacking them so that the first unit sewn is on top again.

- Follow the diagrams to correctly position units for stitching each of the remaining seams to complete Half Log Cabin blocks. Finger press seams away from the Corner Square as you go. Note that the red star ★ indicates that the last log sewn is always in the top position. Make 36.

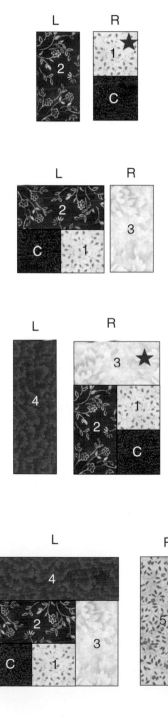

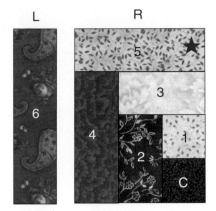

SEWING TIPS

Here are a few hints that will ensure success while sewing the blocks. Note that the order of sewing steps is always the same and guarantees that the blocks will not repeat fabrics in the same positions.

1. Make sure logs and units are correctly positioned, R and L. The diagrams will help.
2. Always position R on top of L, right sides together, and sew the seam along the right edge.
3. Always sew with the log you are adding underneath, closest to the feed dogs. At times this means that you'll need to flip the units over, end for end, in order to keep the new log on the bottom and maintain the direction of seam allowances. This is true for light Logs 3 and 5. Trust me—doing it this way means you won't accidentally sew seam allowances down in the wrong direction. It will make pressing easier and will maintain the scrambled order of logs.
4. Even numbered logs are dark. Saying this will help you remember: "I will even be left in the dark."
5. Odd numbered logs are light. Saying this will help you remember: "Isn't it odd, light rhymes with right."
6. Always press seam allowances away from the Corner Square.

11

Half Log Cabin

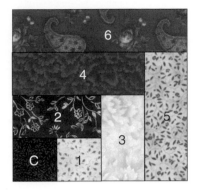

• Press the completed blocks using an iron on a hot setting. You may wish to mist them with spray sizing to make them easier to handle.

ASSEMBLE THE QUILT TOP

• Arrange the blocks in 6 rows of 6 on a design wall (I like using flannel for this) to develop the Barn Raising pattern.

• Sew the blocks into rows. Join the rows to complete the quilt center. Press.

• Measure the length of the quilt. Trim the 2" x 40" inner border print strips to that measurement. Stitch them to opposite sides of the quilt.

• Measure the width of the quilt, including the borders. Trim the 2" x 42" inner border print strips to that measurement. Stitch them to the remaining sides.

• In the same manner, trim the 5" x 42" outer border print strips to fit the quilt's length and stitch them to opposite sides of the quilt.

• Trim the 5" x 52" outer border print strips to fit the quilt's width and stitch them to the remaining sides.

• Complete the quilt as desired, using the 2 1/2" outer border print strips for the binding.

Half Log Cabin Gallery— A Feast for the Eyes!

*I pieced this monochromatic **"Hand-dyed Pinwheels"** (86" x 97") quilt for my son Tom's bed and included a pillow tuck, which is why there are borders on only three sides. Because he doesn't like scrappy quilts made with little flowered prints, I chose gradations of hand-dyed blue fabrics. Placing the 7 1/2" blocks in a pinwheel setting creates a shimmering effect. The spiral machine quilting design further creates a spinning sensation.*

In *"Pink 'n Blue with Geese"* (36" x 50") I selected a single light fabric to use in the 7 1/2" blocks. While both the pink and the blue scrappy blocks each have a controlled color recipe, I stretched the palette by adding peach prints to the pink ones and green prints to the blues. After laying the blocks out in a Field and Furrows setting, I added a pieced border using Flying Geese units left over from another project. To make the borders fit exactly, I trimmed the quilt center evenly on all four sides.

Want to make a few star blocks into a big quilt? I made large Twist 'n Turn blocks using a collection of small star blocks in **"Asilomar Logs"** *(66" square). Then I set them in a modified Sunshine and Shadows layout with Half Log Cabin blocks. My book* Twist 'n Turn *(Chitra Publications, 1998) includes directions for squaring up blocks to a uniform size using my Twist 'n Turn method.*

Half Log Cabin Gallery— A Feast for the Eyes!

*Look at what playing with block layouts can do! Sheryl McConnel used scrappy 6" blocks and came up with this original design for **"Our Back Yard"** (42" square). The pieced braided border sets it off nicely.*

*Carolyn Smith's **"Half Log Cabin Stars"** (66" square) fairly glows. The pieced sashing that creates gold stars across the surface of the quilt and the two sizes of prairie points stitched into the border give her quilt real pizzazz. Carolyn set her blocks in the Sunshine and Shadows layout. She stitched gold squares to the ends of the sashing strips to create the triangular star points, using the same piecing method that is employed for Logs Plus blocks described in Chapter 3.*

Some Pinwheel blocks left over from a workshop found their way into the border of my **"Barn Raising with Pinwheels"** (50" square). I used 2"-wide strips to make 6" blocks. After laying them out, I sewed the blocks in groups of four and added red sashing strips for interest and to brighten the quilt.

"Pattern Play" (65" square) shows what happens to 6" Half Log Cabin blocks made with 2"-wide strips when you play with the layout. The quilt center has a pinwheel effect. The inner border is pieced from quarter-square triangles and enhances the blocks. Colorwise, the scrappy quilt could have gone in any direction. The border fabrics have quite an impact, making a definite color statement.

Half Log Cabin Gallery— A Feast for the Eyes!

*I pieced **"It's a Good Hare Day"** (52" x 66") using 2"-wide strips to make 7 1/2" blocks. A single light fabric is used consistently in all of the blocks. Seven groups of blocks are pieced with scrappy bright strips and each has a specific color recipe. The setting is known as Fields and Furrows. I added some fun with appliqué bunnies from Jeanna Kimball's Fairmeadow design.*

*Scrappy logs look lively in Linda Lardy's **"Streak of Lightning"** (69" x 54"). She used 2"-wide strips to make 7 1/2" blocks. The large-scale floral print in the wide border pulls the quilt together beautifully.*

CHAPTER 3

Logs Plus Quilts

*PROJECT QUILT- **Pinwheel Logs Plus** (50 1/2" square)*

Do you notice anything new in this project quilt? This time blocks contain small contrasting print triangles which are stitched to the dark logs before the blocks are pieced. That's what makes them Logs "Plus" blocks. In my quilt, logs for the light side of the block were cut from assorted pastel yellows. The logs on the dark side were cut from a range of colors, including blues, greens, and lavenders. The squares from which I stitched the triangles were cut from a single contrasting dark blue print. The quilts in the gallery illustrate how bright or contrasting triangles accent the blocks and create a new look for them.

This project is composed of 6" blocks made with 2"-wide strips. Before placing blocks in the Pinwheel setting, I encourage you to play with them on a design wall to see if there is another setting you prefer. You may wish to add a creative touch by changing the border. Study the quilts throughout the book for ideas.

Project Quilt— Pinwheel Logs Plus

QUILT SIZE: 50 1/2" square
BLOCK SIZE: 6" square

MATERIALS

Yardage is based on 44" fabric with a useable width of 42".
- 36 different dark value prints
- 36 different light value prints
- 1/2 yard contrasting accent fabric
- 3/8 yard inner border fabric
- 1 5/8 yards outer border fabric
- 55" square of batting
- 55" square of backing

CUTTING

Dimensions include a 1/4" seam allowance.
- Cut 36: 2" x 19" strips, dark prints
- Cut 36: 2" x 12" strips, light prints
- Cut 9: 2" x 44" strips, accent fabric
- Cut 2: 2" x 44" strips, inner border print
- Cut 2: 2" x 41" strips, inner border print
- Cut 2: 5" x 53" lengthwise strips, outer border print
- Cut 2: 5" x 44" lengthwise strips, outer border print
- Cut 5: 2 1/2" x 44" lengthwise strips, outer border print, for the binding

DIRECTIONS

Precut the logs

Refer to Chapter 1 for more information on precutting as needed.
- Stack 4 dark strips on your cutting mat, rights sides up and long edges aligned. Even the ends, cutting off the selvages.
- Cut these segments from the strips, cutting through all four layers: 2", 3 1/2", 5", 6 1/2". These are Corner Squares and dark logs.

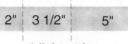

4 dark strips

- Cut segments from the remaining dark strips in the same manner.

- Stack 4 light strips on the mat, aligning and trimming the ends as you did for the dark ones.
- Cut these segments from the strips: 2", 3 1/2", 5". These are light logs.

4 light strips

- Cut segments from the remaining light strips in the same manner.
- Fold one of the 2" x 44" accent strips in fourths. Trim the end and cut through all layers at 2" intervals. Cut the remaining accent strips in the same manner. You will need 144 of these accent squares.

Accent strips

✂ **CUTTING TIP**

Each Logs Plus block requires four 2" squares to make the triangles. For this project you'll make 36 blocks for a total requirement of 4 x 36, or 144 squares. If you plan to make more or fewer blocks for a project, use this formula (4 x Number of Blocks) to determine the number of accent strips you'll need to cut. Each strip yields from 16 to 20 squares, depending on the useable width of your fabric.

Create the triangles on the dark logs

- Lay out the dark logs at the left of your sewing machine with the longest log at the top, as shown.
- Sew a 2" accent square to a 2" dark log with a diagonal seam by first

placing them right sides together, edges aligned. Start sewing where the arrow indicates in the diagram. Stop sewing and leave the unit in the machine with the presser foot down. Use your favorite method for sewing diagonally across the square, or try one outlined for you in the *"Diagonal Seam Tip"* on page 21.
- Chain sew accent squares to the remaining 2" dark logs. Stop sewing and leave the last unit sewn in the machine with the presser foot down. Sew an accent square to a 3 1/2" dark log. Continue chain sewing accent squares to the 3 1/2", 5", and 6 1/2" dark logs, as shown. Be sure to follow the direction of the seam from corner to corner as indicated by the arrow. These are directional units, so consistent sewing is very important.
- Remove the units from the machine. Beginning with the last unit sewn, clip the thread between units and stack them in piles by size. The first unit sewn is now on top of each pile and the wrong side of the accent square shows.

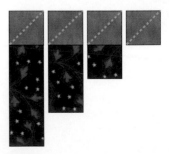

- Finger press the accent fabric toward the corner of each dark log, and stack them as you work so that the first unit sewn is now on the bottom. If done correctly, each stack of 4 pieced logs will have the same dark fabric showing.

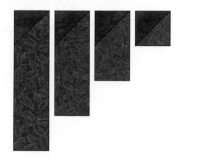

MANAGEABLE PIECING TIP

While I prefer to work with each pile of 4 logs to yield 4 blocks at a time, the scrambling method is the same regardless of how many logs you work with. Try 8 or 16, or even work with all 36 for this project.

SCRAMBLE THE STRIPS

Refer to Chapter 1 for more information on scrambling, as needed.

- Follow the instructions in the diagram to scramble both the light and dark logs. The numbers refer to the positions of each log in the block and the sewing order. "C" refers to the pieced Corner Squares. Note that the pieced Corner Squares and the light squares (Log 1) are not scrambled.

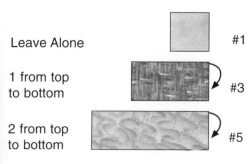

Leave Alone   #1

1 from top to bottom   #3

2 from top to bottom   #5

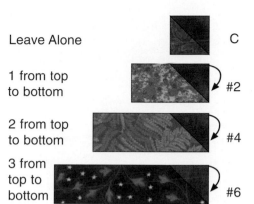

Leave Alone   C

1 from top to bottom   #2

2 from top to bottom   #4

3 from top to bottom   #6

LAY OUT THE BLOCKS FOR SEWING

- Keeping the order of each pile intact, lay out logs for the blocks at the left of your sewing machine, following the diagram. Logs 1, 3, and 5 are light, and Logs 2, 4, and 6 are dark.
- Check the direction of the seamline on the accent triangles. The block always begins with the Corner Square in the lower left. Light logs are all on the right side of the block while dark ones appear on the left side of the block.

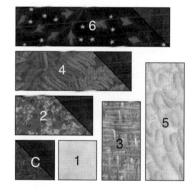

SEW THE BLOCKS

- Take a pieced Corner Square and a 2" light square from the piles and place them in front of the sewing machine as shown in the diagram. Be sure they are positioned so that the pieced Corner Square is on the right (R) and light square (Log 1) is on the left (L).
- Place R on top of L, right sides together. To chain sew units, stitch the squares together and stop, leaving the needle

and presser foot down and the unit in the machine.
- Pick up the next two squares from the same piles and sew them, leaving them in the machine as before. Chain sew the remaining pieced Corner Squares and light squares in the same manner.
- Remove the units from the machine. Beginning with the last unit sewn, clip the thread between units, and stack the unopened units so that the first one sewn is now on top.

- Turn the entire stack over so that the last unit is now on top and the last segment sewn (light Log #1) is visible. Keep the seamline at the top, away from your body.
- Starting with the unit on top, lift light Log 1 to open the unit and finger press the seam allowance toward it (away from the Corner Square). Repeat with the remaining units, stacking them so that the first unit sewn is on top again.
- Follow the diagrams to correctly position units for stitching each of the remaining seams to complete the Logs Plus blocks. Finger press seams away from the Corner Square as you go. Note that the red star ★ indicates that the last log sewn is always in the top position. Make 36.

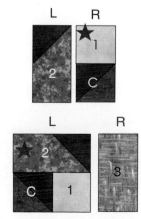

Logs Plus Quilts

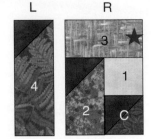

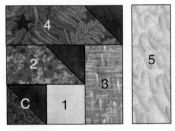

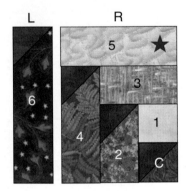

- Press the blocks using an iron on a hot setting. You may wish to mist them with spray sizing to make them easier to handle.

ASSEMBLE THE QUILT TOP

- Arrange the blocks in 6 rows of 6 on a design wall (I like using flannel) to develop the Pinwheel pattern.
- Sew the blocks into rows and join the rows to complete the quilt center. Press.
- Measure the length of the quilt. Trim the 2" x 41" inner border print strips to that measurement. Stitch them to opposite sides of the quilt.
- Measure the width of the quilt, including the borders. Trim the 2" x 44" inner border print strips to that measurement. Stitch them to the remaining sides.
- In the same manner, trim the 5" x 44" outer border print strips to fit the quilt's length and stitch them to opposite sides of the quilt.
- Trim the 5" x 53" outer border print strips to fit the quilt's width and stitch them to the remaining sides.
- Complete the quilt as desired, using the 2 1/2" x 44" outer border print strips for the binding.

TRIMMING TIP: I prefer not to trim away the two underneath layers of the logs and triangles. One reason for leaving them (or at least leaving the dark portion of the log in place) is accuracy. It's easier to keep the units from becoming distorted by pressing if you have the edges of the dark log as a guide. Also, not trimming the units will save you time.

However, if you wish to trim them, cut the two underneath triangles (one accent and one dark log) 1/4" beyond the seamline and discard the excess.

The bulk caused by leaving the underneath layers in place is a problem only if you plan to hand quilt through them. However, because the goal is to make the little triangles "pop," I suggest you quilt around them rather than on them. I've made Logs Plus quilts both ways and find that it isn't possible to tell which units were trimmed and which weren't.

DIAGONAL SEAM TIP

Try any of these methods to sew a perfectly straight and accurate line from corner to corner.

- **Crease a sewing line:**
  Fold each accent square in half diagonally, making a crease from corner to corner. Use the crease as your sewing line.

- **Draw a sewing line:**
  Using a pencil and ruler, lightly mark a sewing line from corner to corner on the wrong side of each accent square.

- **Make a guide**
  Use 1/4"-wide masking tape on the bed of your sewing machine to guide your stitching. Here's how:
  1. Leave the presser foot up and lower the needle into the needle hole of the machine.
  2. Working from the left side of the needle, position a strip-cutting ruler against it.
  3. Lower the presser foot to secure the ruler.

4. Adhere a strip of 1/4"-wide masking tape along the edge of the ruler, starting at the feed dogs and coming toward you as far as the bed of your machine allows. If the tape crosses over the throat plate of your machine so that it may interfere with replacing the bobbin or cleaning the bobbin area, make a slit across the width of the tape along the machine opening.
5. Lift the needle and presser foot to remove the ruler.
6. To use the guide, line up the corner of the accent square closest to you with the left edge of the tape. Keep your eye on this corner rather than on the needle. Sew the seamline, keeping the corner aligned with the edge of the tape as you go. You'll get perfect corner-to-corner sewing every time!

SEWING TIPS

Here are a few hints that will ensure success while sewing the blocks. Note that the order of sewing steps is always the same and guarantees that the blocks will not repeat fabrics in the same positions.

1. Check the direction of the seam when making accent triangles. The units are directional and rely on all of the logs being stitched accurately.
2. Make sure logs and units are correctly positioned, R and L. The diagrams will help.
3. Always position R on top of L, right sides together, and sew the seam along the right edge.
4. Always sew with the log you are adding underneath, closest to the feed dogs. At times this means that you'll need to flip the units over, end for end, in order to keep the new log on the bottom. This is true for light Log 3 and 5. Trust me—doing it this way will make pressing seam allowances easier and will maintain the scrambled order of logs.
5. Even numbered logs are dark. Saying this will help you remember: "I will even be left in the dark."
6. Odd numbered logs are light. Saying this will help you remember: "Isn't it odd, light rhymes with right."
7. Always press seam allowances away from the Corner Square.

8. Explore other design options. For example, what if you placed the dark pieced logs so that all of the triangles are positioned on the left side of the block? What if you assembled blocks so that the small pieced log is in the upper left corner instead of the lower left? You'll see such variations in two of the gallery quilts.

Logs Plus Gallery—
Half Log Cabins and a Bit More

"Barn Raising on Point" (56" square) looks like a blue quilt because of the border fabric. When you study the dark logs, you'll see that there are actually more black and brown fabrics used in them. The bright blue border makes the few blues in the strips more visible.

Margret Reap combined Logs Plus blocks with Half Log Cabin blocks pieced from all light fabric strips to make **"Southwest Variation"** *(70" square). She used green, blue, and peach fabrics for the accent triangles, carefully positioning the blocks to show them off to advantage. Her innovative setting combines Sunshine and Shadows and a modified Barn Raising.*

*"**Something to Crow About**" (56"
square) contains 6" Logs Plus blocks. I
gave it a folk art feel by placing 6"
Uneven Star blocks in the design in place
of some of the Logs Plus blocks. Rather
than four Logs Plus blocks in the center, I
used a 12" appliqué block designed and
made by quilting friend Arlene Stamper.
See how combining other blocks with
Logs Plus creates exciting new looks.*

*I used an original set inspired by
the traditional Barn Raising one
in "**Window of Opportunity**"
(60" square). I also changed the
block construction to create the
variation you see here.*

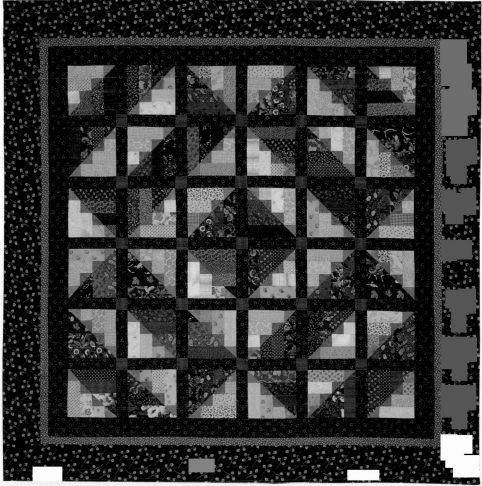

Logs Plus Gallery—
Half Log Cabins and a Bit More

Reproduction prints are right at home in Carolyn Smith's **"30-Something"** (48" x 60"). She used 1930s-look fabrics for the dark half of the block, combining them with clear white on the light side. It's important to note that Carolyn used a variation of the Logs Plus blocks created by turning the logs and keeping the accent triangles on one side of each block. It's fun to explore new ways to work with quilt patterns.

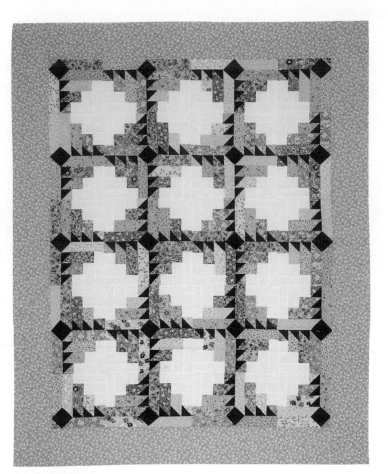

Redwork fan Sandra Munsey made a quilt similar in layout to "Something to Crow About" (page 23). However, in her **"Grand American Barn Garden"** (61" square) she used embroidered redwork blocks with Logs Plus ones. The center floral block is from Charlene Tarbox's Floral Designs and Motifs for Artists (Dover Publications). Other flower blocks represent state flowers and are from State Flowers: Twill-Wick! (Originals by Karen Inc.) The insects are from Sandra's original drawings. Notice how effectively she used Logs Plus strips in the border.

Since becoming a grandmother in 1999, I find that my color palette for quilts is getting brighter and more playful as illustrated in *"Clowning Around"* (60" square). The blocks are a variation of the standard Logs Plus design, and some of them are pieced using all light fabrics. The machine appliquéd clowns were modified from a commercial pattern I purchased in the '80s. Triangles extend into the border for a lively look.

What if you used Logs Plus blocks as a border on another quilt? That's what I did in *"Plaids Plus"* (48" square). Framing the plaid stars set in red sashing made an elaborate-looking yet easy border.

CHAPTER 4

Layout Strategies

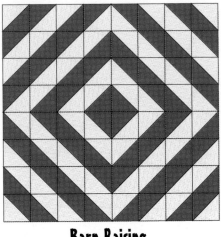
Barn Raising

Fields and Furrows

Streak of Lightning

There are many ways to set your Half Log Cabin and Logs Plus blocks together. Some Log Cabin quilt settings have traditional names such as Barn Raising or Streak of Lightning to describe the layout. The quilts in the previous chapters offer setting ideas, but by no means do they illustrate all of the possibilities.

Because both of these blocks are visually divided in half by the placement of the light and dark fabrics, you have many layout options. (Although the Chevron Log Cabin blocks discussed in the next chapter are usually colored so the logs form "V" bands, you may still be able to use some of the layout ideas presented here for them.) Use the illustrations in this chapter to jump start your creativity. These layouts create very graphic quilt designs. Let them guide you when laying out your blocks, or come up with new arrangements of your own.

A DESIGN WALL

Once your blocks are completed, I encourage you to play with them on a flannel wall. It's a great way to start and there's something really inspiring about seeing all of the blocks up on a vertical surface. I use a neutral color flannel sheet thumb tacked securely on all sides to a wall. Cotton batting can also work well. If you don't have unbroken wall space, improvise by securing flannel to a rigid surface such as a piece of wall board or a large artist's canvas. The flannel or batting-covered surface allows you to position blocks without pinning them. This makes it easy to arrange and rearrange them to find your favorite layout.

HOW MANY BLOCKS?

Many basic Log Cabin layouts are most successful when they contain an even number of blocks in both directions. For example, a Barn Raising-style quilt set in eight rows of six blocks each would look more balanced than if you made it with seven

Geese

Half and Half

X-Cross

Pinwheel

Sunshine and Shadows

Pyramids

rows of five blocks. To demonstrate this concept, look at the Barn Raising diagram which shows eight rows of eight blocks each (8 x 8). Using an index card or your hands, cover the eighth rows and see what happens. There are some layouts such as Fields and Furrows that can be completed with any number of blocks in either direction.

Normally, when I make blocks without a preconceived idea about the setting I'll use, I make enough so that they can be set in even rows. I might make 24, 36 or 80 blocks, so I can set them 4 x 6, 6 x 6, or 8 x 10 respectively. I find it is preferable to have a few blocks left over rather than needing to piece a few more!

STRAIGHT OR ON POINT?

While not many Log Cabin-style quilts have blocks set on point, I'm partial to doing so. "Hand-dyed Pinwheels" on page 12 is set on point in the Pinwheel layout. I love the way the blocks appear to spin when set this way. "Barn Raising on Point" on page 22 is an example of a Logs Plus quilt set this way. Doesn't it make you wonder what Streak of Lightning or Sunshine and Shadows would look like on point? Guess you'll need to make some blocks and put them up on the flannel wall to find out!

If you do select a setting with

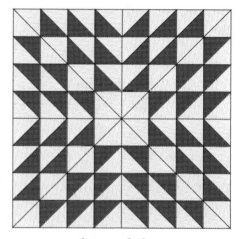

Sawtooth Star

Barn Raising Variation

Barn Raising Variation

Barn Raising Variation

blocks on point, you'll need setting triangles to fill in around the edges of the quilt. These setting pieces are usually cut in two different ways to yield side triangles and corner triangles. Cutting a square diagonally in both directions yields four side triangles. Cutting one in half diagonally yields 2 corner triangles. Doing this keeps the stretchy bias edges of the triangles away from the outside edge of the quilt to avoid distortion.

Since both "Hand-dyed Pinwheels" and "Barn Raising on Point" have corners created by two blocks, I was able to assemble corner units using only side triangles, joining two of them to make a unit. However, there are times when you might want to use a single block at the corners and would need to cut a corner triangle. That's why I've provided a chart on this page that includes dimensions for squares from which you'll cut side and corner triangles when working with various block sizes.

OTHER DESIGN IDEAS

Another uncommon element seen in some of the quilts in this book is sashing. I love the way sashing creates a window-like effect, adding depth to the design. It also allows you to introduce color, either to brighten and intensify the blocks or to soften and separate them. When the blocks are on the flannel wall, you have a perfect opportunity to audition strips of fabric between them to see what effect sashing might have.

Some of the quilts previously shown combine Half Log Cabin and Logs Plus blocks with other ones. Do you already have blocks in your sewing room that might be used this way? You'll find an example of a Chevron quilt in Chapter 5 that also illustrates this design idea.

Use Half Log Cabin and Logs Plus blocks as a border for other blocks. They add more interest than plain strips would, and you can make them quickly. While playing on the design wall, you might try bordering the Half Log Cabin, Logs Plus, or Chevron blocks with ones in other patterns. I used Pinwheel blocks for the Half Log Cabin quilt on page 15. A little pieced tulip block makes a fun border on the Chevron Log Cabin quilt on page 33. Using different blocks in combination with each other enhances both patterns.

SETTING TRIANGLE CHART

Finished Block Size	Cut a square for 4 side triangles	Cut a square for 2 corner triangles
4"	7"	3 3/4"
5"	8 3/8"	4 1/2"
6"	9 3/4"	5 1/8"
6 1/4"	10 1/8"	5 3/8"
7 1/2"	11 7/8"	6 1/4"
9"	14"	7 1/4"

CHAPTER 5

Chevron Log Cabin Quilts

*PROJECT QUILT- "**Scrappy Chevron**" (44 1/8" square)*

The Chevron Log Cabin block is pieced in a way that is similar to the Half Log Cabin and Logs Plus blocks. However, it is usually colored in gradations from light to dark. This results in what resembles "V" bands within the block rather than the split diagonal look of the other two blocks. Traditionally the Chevron block begins with a red Corner Square or one in another bright accent color. Usually the square is the same width as the strips sewn to it, but this is not always the case. Sometimes the square is substantially larger, and other times it's smaller.

Occasionally you'll see a basic Chevron block that is colored so the value of the "V" bands alternates light, dark, light, dark. The traditional layout of Chevron blocks is on point with the corner square at the top.

Of course, these basics are just starting points. You can cut a corner square any size you want and you don't have to use a bright accent fabric for it. You have many options for coloring and block layout. Get ideas from the quilts in the gallery, (pages 32-35) and then play with blocks to come up with your own unique creation.

The Chevron Log Cabin project quilt is a traditional interpretation. Notice that these blocks have logs in eight positions. In addition to the red corner square, each block contains four fabrics. These are shaded from the lightest adjacent to the corner square to the darkest on the outside edges of the block. I worked scrappy when piecing, making each block a little different. I sorted dozens of fabric strips into light, medium, medium-dark, and dark groups. If working with many different fabrics seems overwhelming, you might prefer to use a controlled recipe for your first project. Controlled blocks would simply repeat the same fabrics in each block. You could get by with as few as five fabrics—one for the Corner Square and four prints that range in value from light to dark for the logs. You don't need to scramble the logs as you did for the Half Log Cabin and Logs Plus projects. The project quilt is composed of forty-one 5" blocks made using 1 1/2"-wide strips.

Notice how the blocks appear to float in the center of the quilt without touching the outer border. I achieved this effect by adding a narrow 1"-wide inner border cut from the same light background as the setting triangles.

Project Quilt— Scrappy Chevron

QUILT SIZE: 44 1/8" square
BLOCK SIZE: 5" square

MATERIALS
Yardage is based on 44" fabric with a useable width of 42".
- 1/2 yard bright accent fabric for the Corner Squares and binding
- 41 different light value print strips (each at least 1 1/2" x 6")
- 41 different medium value print strips (each at least 1 1/2" x 8")
- 41 different medium-dark value print strips (each at least 1 1/2" x 10")
- 41 different dark value print strips (each at least 1 1/2" x 12")
- 1/2 yard light background fabric for the setting triangles and inner "float" border
- 1 1/2 yards floral print for the outer border
- 49" square of batting
- 49" square of backing

CONTROLLED BLOCKS TIP
If you choose to work with four fabrics shaded light to dark in addition to the bright accent fabric, here's a buying guide:
- 1/3 yard light print
- 1/2 yard medium print
- 1/2 yard medium-dark print
- 2/3 yard dark print

CUTTING
Dimensions include a 1/4" seam allowance.
- Cut 2: 1 1/2" x 44" strips, accent fabric
- Cut 5: 2 1/2" x 44" strips, accent fabric for the binding
- Cut 41: 1 1/2" x 6" strips, light prints
- Cut 41: 1 1/2" x 8" strips, medium prints
- Cut 41: 1 1/2" x 10" strips, medium-dark prints
- Cut 41: 1 1/2" x 12" strips, dark prints
- Cut 2: 1 1/2" x 40" strips, light background fabric for the inner border
- Cut 2: 1 1/2" x 42" strips, light background fabric for the inner border
- Cut 4: 8 3/8" squares, light background fabric, then cut them in quarters diagonally to yield 16 side triangles

- Cut 2: 4 1/2" squares, light background fabric, then cut them in half diagonally to yield 4 corner triangles

- Cut 2: 4" x 49" lengthwise strips, floral print, for the outer border
- Cut 2: 4" x 42" lengthwise strips, floral print, for the outer border

DIRECTIONS
Precut the logs
Refer to Chapter 1 for more information on precutting as needed.
- Stack four 1 1/2" x 6" light strips on your cutting mat, right sides up and edges aligned.
- Cut these segments from the strips, cutting through all four layers: 1 1/2" and 2 1/2". These are logs for Positions 1 and 2.

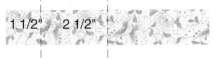

1 1/2"   2 1/2"

4 light strips

- Cut segments from the remaining light strips in the same manner, keeping strips in groups of 4. NOTE: *One strip will be left to cut by itself. Or, include it in one of the groups of 4, making 5 layers to cut through. This will be true when precutting all of the logs for this project.*
- Repeat, stacking groups of 4 medium strips in the same manner and cutting 2 1/2" and 3 1/2" segments from them. These are logs for Positions 3 and 4.
- Cut 3 1/2" and 4 1/2" segments from the 41 medium-dark strips in the same way. These are logs

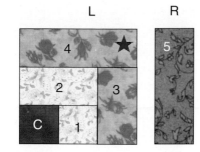

for Positions 5 and 6.

- Cut 4 1/2" and 5 1/2" segments from the 41 dark strips in the same way. These are logs for Positions 7 and 8.

- Fold one of the 1 1/2" x 44" accent strips in fourths. Trim the ends and cut through all layers at 1 1/2" intervals. Cut the remaining accent strip in the same manner. You will need 41 of these accent squares.

LAY OUT THE BLOCKS FOR SEWING

- Lay out logs for the blocks at the left of your sewing machine, following the diagram. "C" is the accent fabric Corner Square, and the logs are numbered in stitching order. The logs are graded from lightest in positions 1 and 2, to darkest in positions 7 and 8.

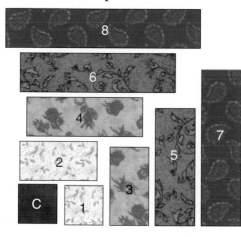

SEW THE BLOCKS

- Take a Corner Square and a 1 1/2" light square from the piles and place them in front of the sewing machine as shown. Be sure they are positioned so that the Corner Square is on the right (R) and the light square (Log 1) is on the left (L).

- Place R on top of L, right sides together. To chain **R** sew units, stitch the squares together and stop, leaving the presser foot down and the unit in the machine.

- Pick up the next two squares from the same piles and sew them, leav-

ing them in the machine as before. Chain sew the remaining Corner Squares and light squares in the same manner.

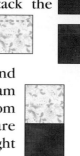

- Remove the units from the machine and clip the threads between them. Stack the unopened units with the light squares up.

- Open each unit and finger press the seam allowance away from the Corner Square and toward the light square.

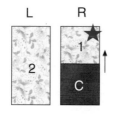

- Follow the diagrams to correctly position units for stitching each of the remaining seams to complete the Chevron blocks. Note that the red star ★ indicates that the last unit sewn is always in the top position. Make 41.

- Press the blocks using an iron on a hot setting. You may wish to mist them with spray sizing to make them easier to handle.

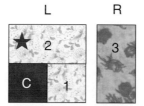

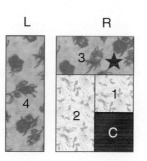

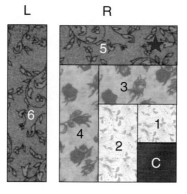

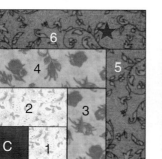

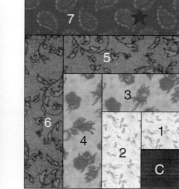

ASSEMBLE THE QUILT TOP

- Arrange the blocks on point on a design wall, filling in with the side and corner triangles. Refer to the quilt photo on page 29 as needed.

- Sew the blocks and triangles into diagonal rows and join the rows to complete the quilt center. Press.

- Measure the length of the quilt. Trim the 1 1/2" x 40" light background strips to that measurement. Stitch them to opposite sides of the quilt.

- Measure the width of the quilt, including the borders. Trim the 1 1/2" x 42" light background strips to that measurement. Stitch them to the remaining sides.

- In the same manner, trim the 4" x 42" floral print strips to fit the quilt's length and stitch them to opposite sides of the quilt.

- Trim the 4" x 49" floral print strips to fit the quilt's width and stitch them to the remaining sides.

- Complete the quilt as desired, using the 2 1/2" x 44" accent strips for the binding.

SEWING TIPS

Here are a few hints that will ensure success while sewing the blocks.

1. Make sure logs and units are correctly positioned, R and L. The diagrams will help.
2. Always position R on top of L, right sides together, and sew the seam along the right edge.
3. Always sew with the log you are adding underneath, closest to the feed dogs. When stitching Logs 3, 5, and 7, flip the unit over, end for end, before stitching. This way you won't sew seam allowances down in the wrong direction.
4. Always press seam allowances away from the Corner Square.
5. Refer to Chapter 2 to devise an organized way to maintain placement of specific fabrics while sewing if this is your goal. This is not a concern when working scrappy.

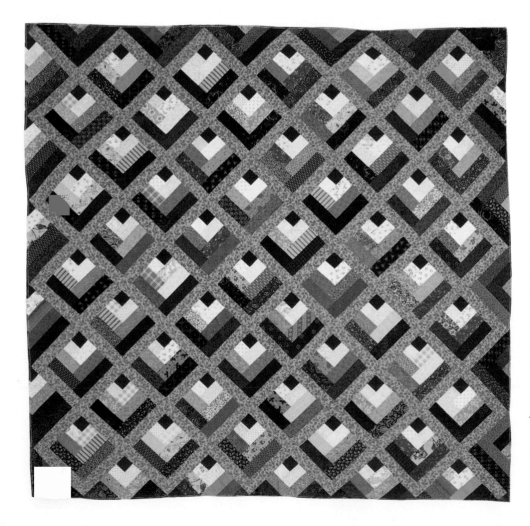

Linda Packer pieced "Sashed Chevron" (61" square) using 2"-wide strips to make 6" blocks. The scrappy blocks with gold sashing give the quilt an antique look. While her quilt is similar to this chapter's Project Quilt, there are a few variations. Of course the sashing and the number of blocks are obvious differences. Notice also that the blocks in Linda's quilt are pieced with wider strips and have fewer log positions (six) than the Project Quilt (eight). She also created pieced setting triangles and finished the quilt without borders.

Although *"Floral Chevron"* (61" square) is a soft, scrappy quilt, Laurine Leeke controlled several things in the quilt's layout. She joined her blocks into groups of four, including two identical blocks in each foursome. Two blocks have Corner Squares placed at the center of each foursome while two are placed at the outside edge. The foursomes are sashed with light strips. The eight setting triangles are pieced from blocks containing the same floral print that's in the border. The quilt has the look of a Lover's Knot design.

A quilting friend gave me 6" Tulip blocks made several years ago using a Mary Ellen Hopkins design. After making the 12 Chevron blocks, I began looking for a way to jazz them up. While searching through my block box, I found the tulip blocks and placed them deliberately, adding sashing to make *"Tulip Dance"* (48" square). It's perfect for spring decorating!

Chevron Gallery— A Lively Look

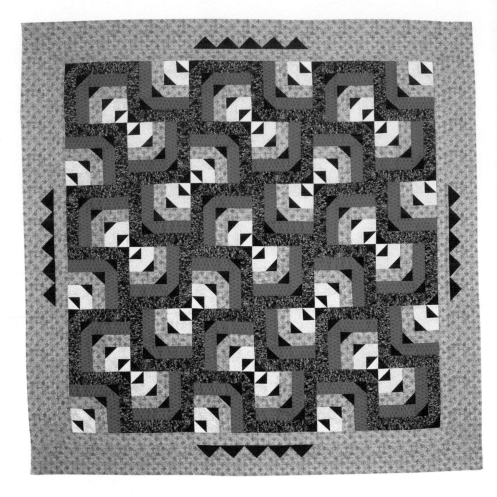

Cher Chu made an exciting Chevron variation for **"Amber Waves"** (58" square). She used a controlled color recipe in her 7 1/2" blocks and added accent triangles like those used in Logs Plus. She cut the logs from 2"-wide strips. Cher added a surprise by inserting some folded prairie points in the borders.

Look closely at the blocks in **"The Fishes Point of View"** (50" square) by Marnie Santos, and you'll see how she varied the strip widths within the block. She also used strips for logs that are similar in value. The border is pieced with three strips—a "floating" narrow background inner, a narrow accent middle, and a wide outer border.

"Chevron Whimsy" (26" square) features faces in the large Corner Squares and varied strip widths in the 6" blocks. Carolyn Smith embellished it with a kite tail and some fun buttons, including smiley faces. This little creation is guaranteed to make anyone smile. Can't you just picture this quilt hanging from the ceiling of a child's room?

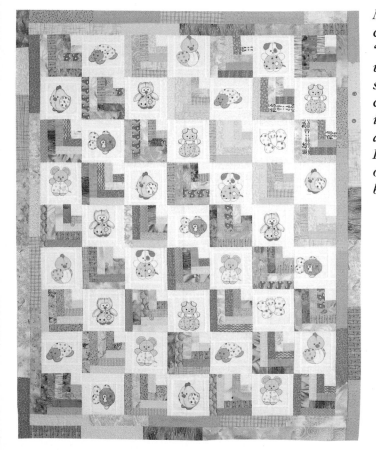

Margret Reap used a controlled color plan but did not concern herself with value placement when making *"Critters 'n Chevrons"* (45" x 56"). The 5 1/2" blocks were made with 2" Corner Squares and 1 1/2"-wide strips for the logs. She found the motifs in a computer clip art program and printed them on fabric using her ink-jet printer. Light tone-on-tone fabric frames them and makes them the same size as the Chevron blocks. Deliberate placement of the colored blocks creates diagonal bands of color across the quilt. Leftover strips became the pieced border.

Sandy Andersen had fun with black and white prints and bright fabrics when piecing the 4 1/2" blocks for *"Lively Chevrons"* (40" x 54"). Each block has logs in four positions. Sandy elected not to work with the traditional light-to-dark shading, but rather in an as-the-spirit-moved-her approach. Once the blocks were completed, she played with them on the design wall and came up with this delightful Rail Fence look. Strategic color placement contributes to the success of her quilt.

CHAPTER 6

Bonus! Foundation Miniature Quilts

Making miniature quilts is becoming increasingly popular, as is foundation piecing. All of the Half Log Cabin variations presented in this book can be made for small-scale quilts.

Foundation piecing is a method that provides accuracy when working with small pieces. This chapter includes eight foundation patterns for blocks ranging from 1 1/2" to 3" square. If you are unfamiliar with the construction technique, you may wish to consult a book such as *Favorite Foundation Pieced Minis* (Chitra Publications, 1999) or *Miniature Quilts* magazine for step-by-step directions. Let the gallery of nine charming mini quilts inspire you. Even small fabric scraps find a home in these little quilts.

Half Log Cabin and Chevron Log Cabin Foundations

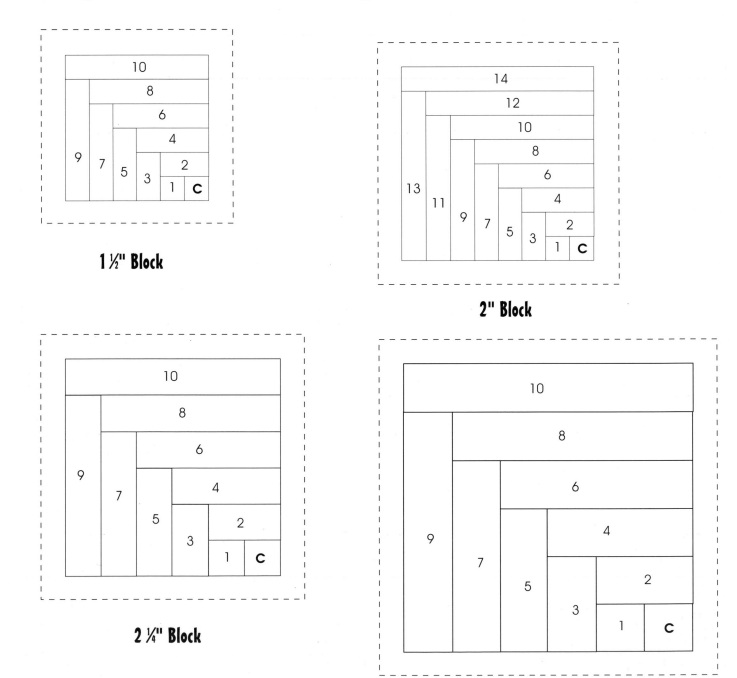

1 ½" Block

2" Block

2 ¼" Block

3" Block

Logs Plus Foundations

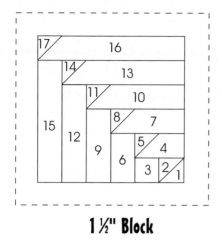

1 ½" Block

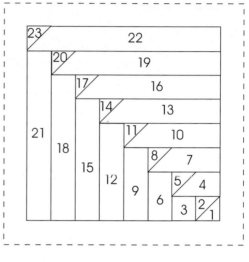

2" Block

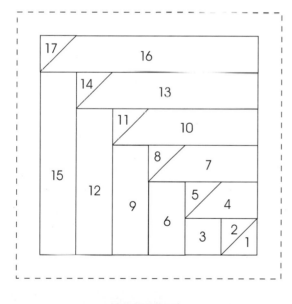

2 ¼" Block

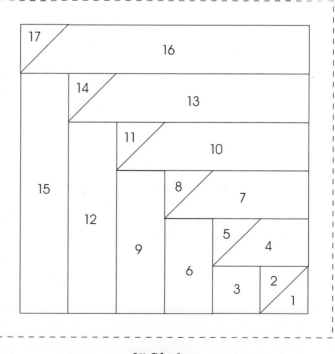

3" Block

Miniature Quilts—
Have a Little Fun with Easy Piecing.

*Miniature Half Log Cabin blocks became the center medallion in Stevii Graves' **"Round Robin"** (30" square), a border exchange quilt.*

***"Live Wire"** (11" square) explodes with color. Quiltmaker Ruth Gordy used Logs Plus blocks in a Sunshine and Shadows setting.*

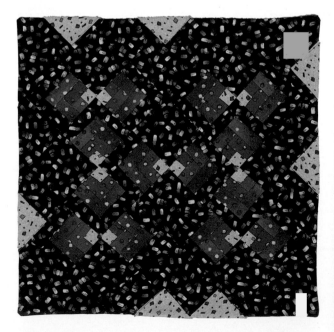

***"Party Time"** (12" square) by Ruth Gordy is pieced from Chevron blocks set in an original design.*

*"**Night and Day**" (8 1/2" x 11") is my quick-to-stitch miniature project. It contains just eight Half Log Cabin blocks set on point and bordered with a floral print.*

*Ruth Gordy used a controlled color recipe for her "**Logs Plus Barn Raising**" (10" square), a miniature with strong contrast. The blocks are set straight.*

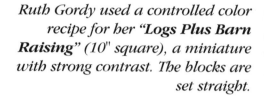

*Sue Haskins pieced 64 little Half Log Cabin blocks and arranged them in a traditional setting. Her "**Sunshine and Shadows Miniature**" (18" square) is the lively result.*

Miniature Quilts—
Have a Little Fun with Easy Piecing.

Bright accent triangles and a rick-rack border give my *"Logs Plus Barn Raising On Point"* (12" square) eye appeal.

I used an array of dark and light fabrics to make this scrappy *"Fields and Furrows Half Log Cabin"* (11" x 13").

Stevii Graves combined the Chevron color placement with black Logs Plus triangles when piecing the 24 blocks for *"Chevron Plus"* (17" x 22") She joined groups of four like-colored blocks and set them straight.

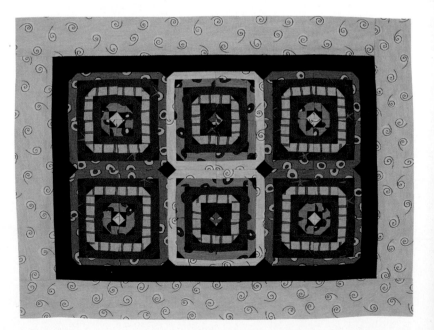